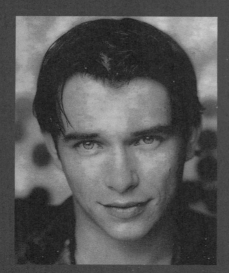

picture of you... 4   baby can i hold you... 14   all that i need... 9   must have been high... 18
and i... 24   that's how love goes... 29   where did you go?... 34   i'm learning (part one)... 40
one kiss at a time... 45   while the world is going crazy... 50   this is where i belong... 60
will be yours... 55   good conversation... 66   you flew away... 73   i'm learning (part two)... 78

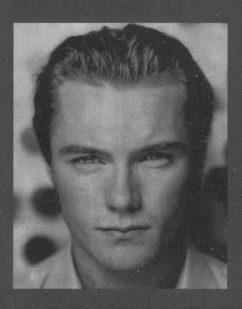

Picture Of You

Words & Music by Eliot Kennedy, Ronan Keating, Paul Wilson & Andy Watkins

the friend— that was there— all a - long?—

Instrumental ad lib.

7

Verse 2:
Do you believe that after all that we've been through
I'd be able to put my trust in you?
Goes to show you can forgive and forget
Looking back I have no regrets, cos

You were with me there *etc.*

8

All That I Need

Words & Music by Evan Rogers & Carl Sturken

1. I was lost and a-lone,____ try-ing to grow,
(Verse 2 see block lyric)

____ mak-ing my way____ down that long____ wind-ing road.____ Had no rea-son or rhyme

Verse 2:

I was searching in vain, playing your game
Had no-one else but myself left to blame
You came into my world, no diamonds or pearls
Could ever replace what you gave to me girl
Just like a castle of sand
Girl I almost let love
Slip right out of my hand
And just like a flower needs rain
I will stand by your side
Through the joy and the pain.

You're the air that I breathe *etc.*

Baby Can I Hold You

Words & Music by Tracy Chapman

14

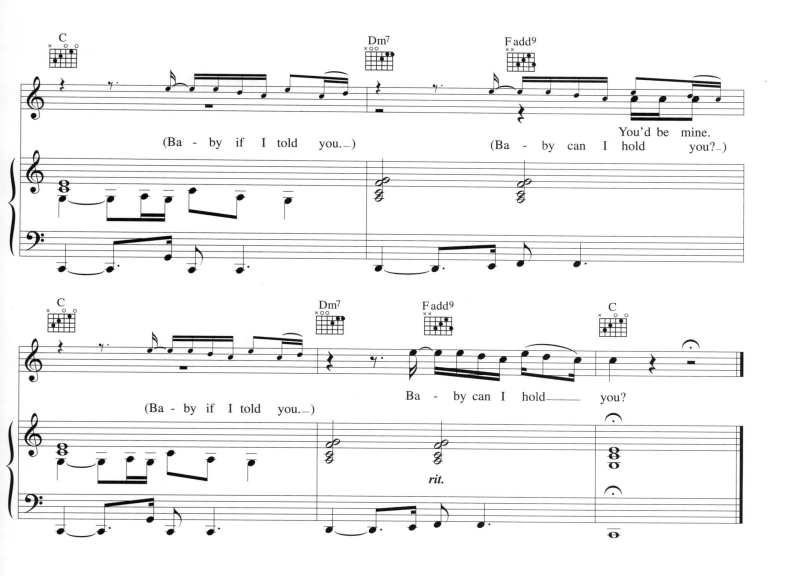

Verse 2:
Forgive me is all that you can't say
Years gone by and still
Words don't come easily
Like forgive me, forgive me.

Verse 3:
I love you is all that you can't say
Years gone by and still
Words don't come easily
Like I love you, I love you.

Must Have Been High

Words & Music by Eric Foster-White

I thought it would be ea-sy and soon you would for-give.

But now I got-ta beg— you girl,— can't stand to be— a-part. And I must-'ve been

high girl,— to let— you— by, no— good rea-son—

why there's— no you and I.— And I must-'ve been

19

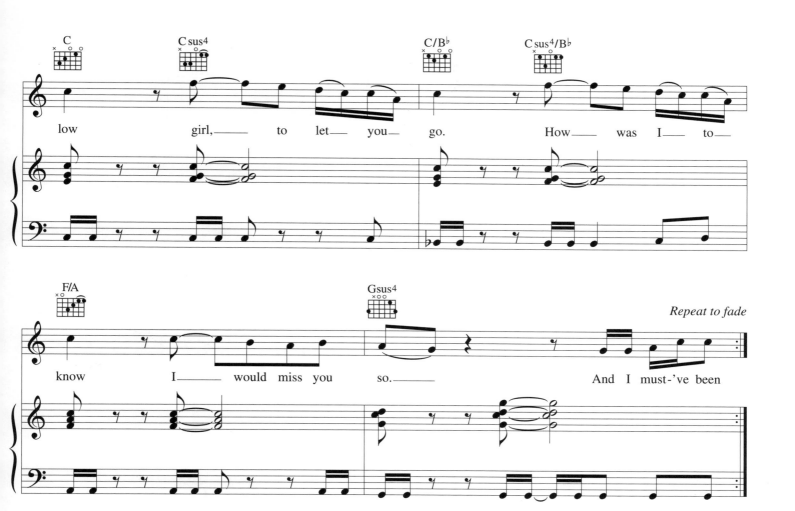

low   girl,   to let you   go.   How   was I   to

Repeat to fade

know   I   would miss you   so.   And I must-'ve been

Verse 2:
I wanted to move on girl
No time to settle down
Didn't wanna give my love to only you.
But since you have been gone girl
I took a look around
And if I gotta beg you girl
That's what I'm gonna do.

And I must've been high *etc.*

And I

Words & Music by Steve Mac, Wayne Hector & Alistair Tennant

1. It's been a while, how have you been do-ing?
(Verse 2 see block lyric)

D'ya ev-er think a-bout_ me and you and_ all the things we used_ to do,_____ the

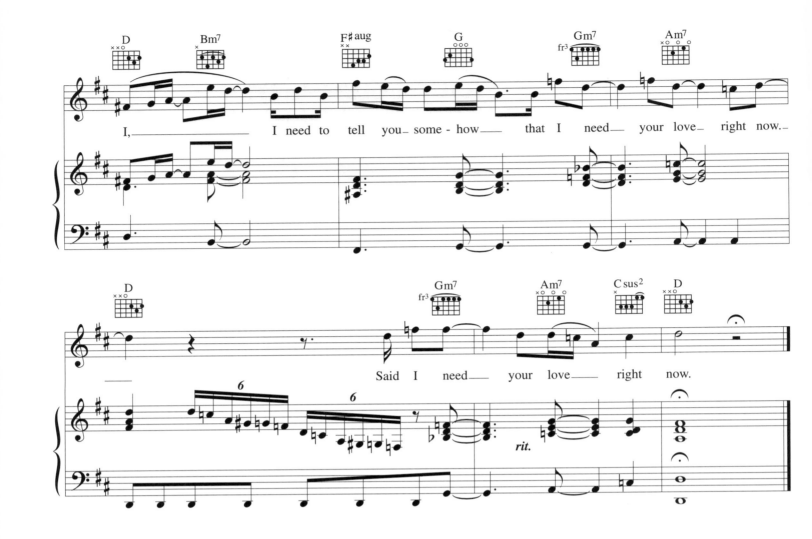

Verse 2:
Looking back I can see things clearly
The mistakes that I paid for dearly
Taking love for granted only leaves you alone.
Well if we talked you would understand
That time has made me a better man
And with your love behind me there's nowhere I can't go
So take a chance. (Just take a chance on me.)
And you'll see. (It's where you need to be.)
If your heart it tells you so
You'll know what I know.

I think of you *etc.*

That's How Love Goes

Words & Music by Steve Booker & Julian Gallagher

1. How ma-ny times have I told you to-night, there's no need to wor-ry,
(Verse 2 see block lyric)

it-'ll all be al-right.— So don't walk a-way, at the end of the day———

I won't make you sor - ry if you de - cide— to stay. Some-times it's hard— to hold on,

that's when your heart needs to be strong.— That's how

love— goes, don't ask me why.— On - ly love— knows— what you're

feel-ing in - side.— That's how love— goes, one day it's— good - bye— then it's

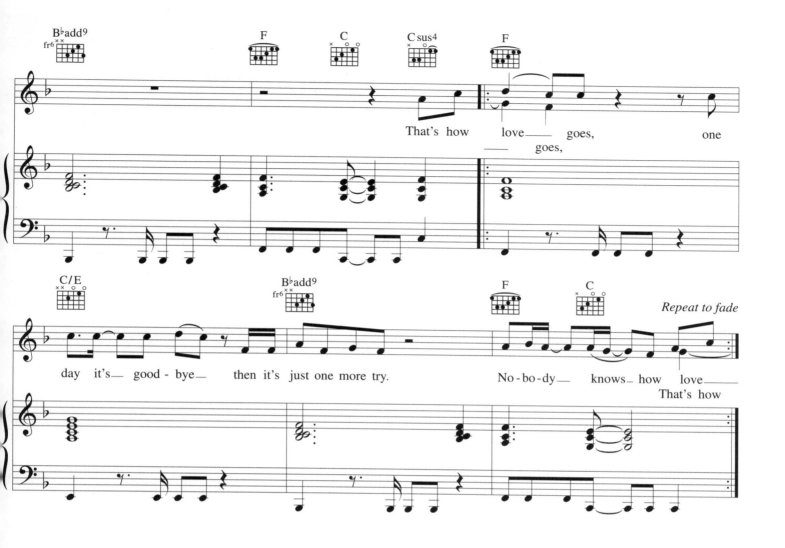

That's how love goes, one goes,
day it's good-bye then it's just one more try. No-bo-dy knows how love
That's how

Repeat to fade

Verse 2:
The more that I see
The more I believe
That nothing is certain
When you're following your dreams.
So all I can do
Is keep holding you
Baby, together
We can make them dreams come true.
Sometimes it's hard to hold on
That's when your heart needs to be strong.

That's how love goes *etc.*

Where Did You Go?

Words & Music by Steve Mac, Stephen Gately, Wayne Hector & Alistair Tennant

Verse 2:
You said forever, we'd cherish all our dreams together
Seems like forever, forever since I felt the pleasure
Oh girl, the pleasure holding you so close at night
The times we used to talk by candle light
There's something in the air you've been so cold
Is there something that I need to know?

Tell me where did you go? *etc.*

I'm Learning (Part One)

Words & Music by Ronan Keating, Ray Hedges & Martin Brannigan

So I'll shed— my tears— and I'll face— my fears,—

I've been told———— there'll be an-oth-er,

so I guess— I'm still lone - ly.————————

Verse 2:
Our cry for help will sound the same now baby
I now know that people just don't change
But I guess you can't hope and wish they will, yeah
So I wanna put my heart in its place
And I wanna be the person that you fell in love with.

I've been told *etc.*

One Kiss At A Time

Words & Music by Evan Rogers, Carl Sturken & Ronan Keating

Soon-er or la - ter love's gon-na get__ you.__ No way that you__ can hide.__

One kiss at a time.__ Mi - nute by mi - nute, hour__ by hour__

1.

I'm gon - na make__ you mine.__ One kiss at a time.__

2, ℅.

Hey now,__ hey now,__ can't be - lieve the way I

feel now,— feel now.— One kiss at a time.— Hey now,— hey now,— can't you feel it when it's

real now,— real now.— One kiss at a time.—

Ooh!——

To Coda

D.%. al Coda

Do do do— do do.——

48

Coda

Soon-er or la - ter   love's gon - na get __ you. __   No way that you __ can   hide. __

__ One   kiss   at   a   time. __   Mi - nute   by   mi - nute,   hour __   by   hour __

I'm gon - na   make __ you   mine. __   One   kiss   at   a   time. __   One kiss   at   a   time. __

Verse 2:
In all of the heavens
You're the only star that shines
I've just gotta get to you
So I'm workin' overtime.
I've climbed every mountain
Just to show you that I care
The searchin' is done
And girl you're the one
I'm gonna take you there.

One kiss at a time *etc.*

While The World Is Going Crazy

Words & Music by Evan Rogers, Carl Sturken & Ronan Keating

safe and warm in-side. Close the door and for-get a-bout time,

ease the riv-er run-nin' through your mind. Lay your bo-dy next to me, let your

se-crets all be mine. Take my hand and be-lieve me that love will guide us through.

An-y time that you need me girl, I'll be there for you. While the

52

Verse 2:
I turned on the news today
But I don't wanna hear a word they say
Outside the world is breakin' down
But we don't have a clue.
Like a scream in an empty room
It's getting harder just to find the truth
Let's forget it 'til the night is through
It's not about me and you.
We can make our own heaven
It's not so hard to find
'Cause girl I will protect you
Until the end of time.

While the world *etc.*

Will Be Yours

Words & Music by Jorgen Elofsson, Pete James, Per Magnusson & David Kreuger

1. Look here now, read my lips fo - cus on my fin - ger tips,
(Verse 2 see block lyric)

un - der - stand these op - en hands. I give to you all that's true. So

sail a - way and free your ghost. Give to whom you love the most.

Give a - way and you'll be - lieve all good things you'll re - The

Verse 2:
If I'm the one you're looking for
Then open up that bolted door
Let me in and lead me through
You know I'll do the the same for you
Step by step you'll be aware
Heart to heart if truth is there
Now give away and you'll believe
All good things you'll receive.

The more you give *etc.*

This Is Where I Belong

Words & Music by Evan Rogers, Carl Sturken & Ronan Keating

1. Here I stand in the North-ern rain and I can't be-lieve I'm home a - gain.

(Verse 2 see block lyric)

And I can't be-lieve how noth-ing's changed, I'm find-ing my way.

Old park bench on where I carved my name, but

now it does-n't stand a - lone, 'cause now the trees have ov - er - grown.

Ma-ny a road that I've tra-velled that's led me a-stray,

here's where my heart's gon - na stray. This is where I

be - long, this is where I come from.

No need to shed my tears or face my fears an-y-more.

Oh, oh. So I won't walk a - lone,

tak-ing things on my own. All of the lands

Verse 2:
There you stood in the open door
Just like so many years before
When I told you that I needed more
In my life.
I was wrong to ever walk away
Abandon all the love that we made
But now I've learned from all my mistakes
Just like a star in the sky
Guiding me on
Your love is pulling me home.

This is where I belong. _etc._

Good Conversation

Words & Music by Steve Mac, Mikey Graham & Wayne Hector

D.%. al Coda

Verse 3 (𝄋):
Every day I'm surrounded by
A million voices from the sky
And they all have the same thing to say.
Now what I need is something new
Is it something you can do
To share in that kind of good conversation?
It's good conversation that puts my mind at ease.

You Flew Away

Words & Music by Stephen Gately

Verse 2:
Sat along the bay
Watched the stars in the sky
Seems like yesterday
That you were by my side.
And if I could give
Would you still want me
And would you forgive
Oh why did you have to go out of my life?
Never got the chance to say goodbye.

You flew away *etc.*

I'm Learning (Part Two)

Words & Music by Ronan Keating, Ray Hedges & Martin Brannigan

1. How is it now,   have you moved on?
(Verse 2 see block lyric)

And do you still think of me   when I'm—

—— gone?

I think of you   and I just won - der——

Verse 2:
It's so simple to say I love you
But sometimes it's just not enough
So I'll find my sunrise
At the end of these few words.

Who are you holding now *etc.*